To Be a Kid

Maya Ajmera and John D. Ivanko

D0503504

NATIONAL GEOGRAPHIC
Hampton-Brown

When you are a kid, you spend time with your family.

Portugal

Canada

Nepal

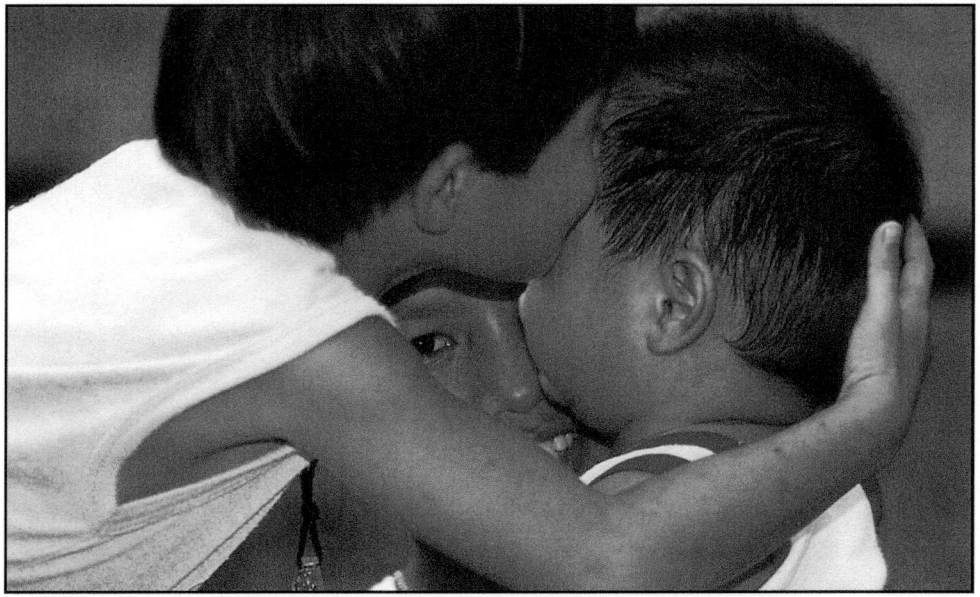

Philippines

Israel

Senegal

You go places

Nepal

with people who love you.

Japan

United States

You go to school

South Africa

Pakistan

Russia

and learn lots of new things.

Philippines

Ethiopia

Marshall Islands

You walk home together,

South Africa

share a story,

Guatemala

Ecuador

have a cool snack on a summer day,

Denmark

Bolivia

or march in a parade.

Ecuador

United States

Botswana

you play ball,

India

Cuba

Mexico

Antigua and Barbuda

run races,

Mexico

France

go skating,

Switzerland

Sweden

ride a merry-go-round,

Austria

or play a board game.

Nepal

France

United States

You paint beautiful pictures,

South Africa

Poland

share the joy of music,

Peru

China

or dance your heart out.

Philippines

Ireland

India

United States

United Kingdom

You take care of animals.

United States

Japan

India

Haiti

Mongolia

Ecuador

You goof off

Madagascar

South Africa

and act silly.

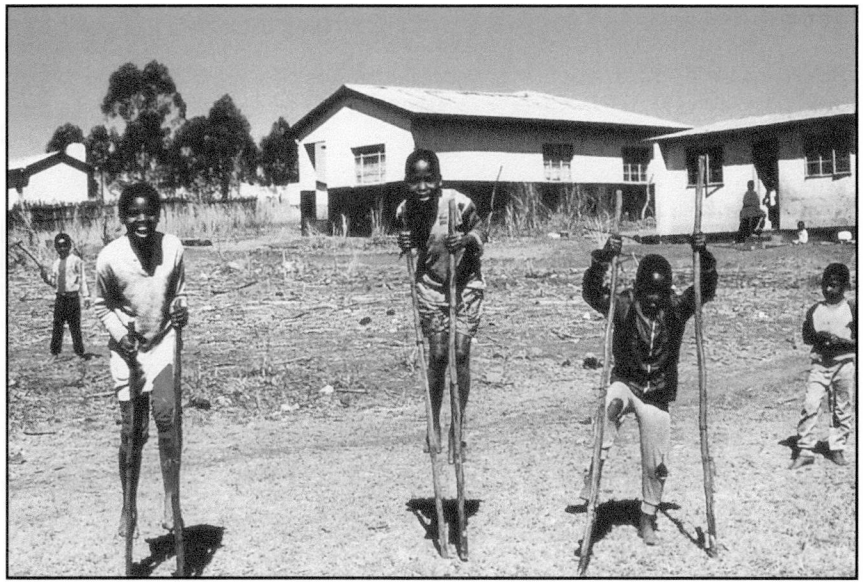

Swaziland

Guatemala

Belize

When you are a kid, you make friends

China

Benin

Australia

that last forever and ever.

Oman

Mozambique

United States